THE
REAL
USA

Your need-to-know guide for all things American

Jackson Teller

FRANKLIN WATTS
LONDON•SYDNEY

First published in 2013
by Franklin Watts

Copyright © Franklin Watts 2013

Franklin Watts
338 Euston Road
London NW1 3BH

Franklin Watts Australia
Level 17/207 Kent Street
Sydney, NSW 2000

Series Editor: Sarah Peutrill
Series Designer: Sophie Wilkins
Picture Researcher: Diana Morris

Dewey number: 917.3

HB ISBN: 978 1 4451 1971 7
Library ebook ISBN: 978 1 4451 2598 5

Printed in China

Franklin Watts is a division of Hachette Children's
Books, an Hachette UK company.
www.hachette.co.uk

Picture credits: age footstock/Robert Harding
PL: 30tl, 33. AlaskaStock/Alamy: 38. Dave Allen/
Shutterstock: 42tc. American Spirit/Dreamstime:
30c. amygdala-imagen/istockphoto: 37.
Apple Corp.: 17b. Bayda127/Dreamstime: 13t,
42tr. Charles Brutlag/Shutterstock: 20tr, 21bl.
Andriano Castelli/Shutterstock: 5c, 12. Jayne
Chapman/Shutterstock: 42tl. col/Shutterstock:
6tr, 40t, 47. dibrova/istockphoto: 15b. Dennis
Donohue/Shutterstock: 35. C Flannigan/
WireiMage/Getty Image: 24c. Jorg Hackmann /
Shutterstock: 42b. Janaph/Shutterstock: 34b.
Ritu Manoj Jethani/Shutterstock: 24tr, 29c.
joyfuldesigns/Shutterstock: 5tr, 6c, 30tr, 32.
Kim Karpeles/Alamy: 27. Andrew F. Kazmierski/
Shutterstock: 10b. Kojihirano/Shutterstock: 7, 36.
Kokophoto/istockphoto: 34t. Vladimir
Korostyshevskiy/Dreamstime: 18t. Radoslaw
Lecyk/Shutterstock: 6tl,10t. Katrina Leigh/
Shutterstock: 9. Lvphotog1/Dreamstime:
front cover bc. Lissandra Melo/Shutterstock :
11b, 16tc, 18b. meunierd/Shutterstock: 43.
Aleksandar Mijatovic/Shutterstock: front cover br.
Monkey Business Images/Shutterstock: 20tl, 22.
mountainberryphoto/istockphoto: front cover
t. Ron Niebrugge/Alamy: 29b. Jim Parkin/
Shutterstock: 5tc, 8t, 48. Douglas Peebles/Alamy:
5b, 40b. Beniot Rousseau/istockphoto: 39.
Mario Savola/Shutterstock: 2, 13b. Phillip Scalia/
Alamy: 14. Joe Seer/Shutterstock: 5tl, 24tc, 28c.
Andy Shepherd/Redferns/Getty Images: 26.
Paul Simon/Cultura/Alamy: 41.Steve Skjold /
Alamy: 20c. Spirit of America/Shutterstock: 16tl,
19. Jeremy Sterk/istockphoto: 20tc, 23. Phillip
Stidh/Shutterstock: 21br. Vaclav/Shutterstock:
24tl, 28t. Vic36/Dreamstime: front cover bl.
Volina/Shutterstock: 8b. wdstock/istockphoto:
15t. Wisconsinart/Shutterstock: 30tc, 31.
Danny Xu/ Shutterstock: 1, 6tc, 11t. Zolta_11/
Shutterstock: 25.

Every attempt has been made to clear copyright.
Should there be any inadvertent omission please
apply to the publisher for rectification.

CONTENTS

New York, p.12

INTRODUCING THE USA

What's hot: USA	6
Facts and stats	8
People	10

NEW YORK

New York, N.Y.	12
Shopping – the inside guide	14

TECHNOLOGY AND TRANSPORT

Apple crazy!	16
Car crazy!	18

FOOD AND FESTIVALS

America's favourite foods	20
Thanksgiving: The USA's No. 1 holiday	22

CULTURE

Music map of America	24
Music festivals	26
L.A. and Hollywood	28

SPORT

National sports	30
A day at the rodeo	32

ON AN ADVENTURE

A visit to the super-volcano	34
Rafting the Grand Canyon	36
Alaska	38
The Hawaiian Islands	40

THE ESSENTIALS

Key information for travellers	42
Finding out more	45
Index	46

Hawaii, p.40

WHAT'S HOT: USA

Rodeo, p. 32

The USA is an amazingly varied country. Whether you want exciting cities, beautiful landscapes, extreme sports or something else, you will probably be able to find it here. These are just a few of the highlights you can discover more about later in this book.

1. HALLOWEEN PARADE, WASHINGTON SQUARE p.12

Thousands of people in Halloween costumes (about 50,000, in fact) mix with musicians, circus performers, magicians and dancers in a crazy parade through the heart of Manhattan. Watch out for the giant puppets, moved by teams of puppeteers using long rods.

2. SOUTH BY SOUTHWEST p.26

This is one of the USA's best music festivals, with live acts playing all around the city of Austin, Texas. There are also film and interactive media festivals going on at the same time.

3. HAUNTED TOUR OF LOS ANGELES p.29

You COULD take a tour of houses where famous movie stars have lived, or a guided trip around one of the studios. But this spooky haunted-locations tour is a bit different. Maybe you'll even hear the ghostly movie-star trumpeter at the Hollywood Roosevelt Hotel.

4. VISIT TO THE RODEO p.32

Cowboy boots, Stetson hats, check shirts – and that's just the audience. You should see the rodeo riders! The modern-day rodeo is a Wild West feast of cowboy (and girl) skills, music and food.

5. THE NAKED BIKE RIDE p.19

In most of the USA, the car is king. In Portland, Oregon, the bicycle is starting to take over. To prove it, the city hosts a Naked Bike Ride, in which thousands of overexcited, under-dressed riders pedal through the city centre.

6. RAFTING THE GRAND CANYON p.36

One of the USA's most famous natural attractions, the Grand Canyon, is 446 km long and up to 29 km wide. What better way to see it than to raft down the lower section, paddling by day and camping on the bank at night?

7. THE BIRTHPLACE OF SURFING p.41

Some 3,800 km off the west coast of the USA are the Hawaiian Islands. This is where the sport of surfing was born, when great Hawaiian chiefs and warriors learned the art of standing up on a wooden surfboard. Today, you don't have to be a great chief to try surfing – everyone is allowed.

The Grand Canyon, p.36

IT'S (NEARLY) OFFICIAL!
TOP PLACES TO VISIT IN THE USA

Members of one of the world's biggest travel websites picked these top US destinations:

1. New York City – if the USA's biggest city feels a bit like a film set, it's because you've already seen the streets on screen so many times.

2. San Francisco – on one of the world's most beautiful natural harbours, this hilly city is great for simply wandering around.

3. Chicago – great for foodies; one of the best ways to see Chicago is to take an architectural tour of the centre – by boat.

4. Honolulu – with its mix of American, Pacific and Asian culture, Honolulu is a fascinating place to visit.

5. Los Angeles – take a tour of Hollywood, visit a film studio, hang out on the beach or just sit in a café and watch the cool-cat Californians float by.

6. New Orleans – the French-influenced city's unofficial motto is *Laisser les bon temps rouler* – let the good times roll.

USA FACTS AND STATS

There's no getting away from it: the USA is a BIG country. You could fit all 27 countries of the European Union into the USA – twice! Whether you want buzzing cities, rocky landscapes, palm-fringed beaches or wide-open plains, the USA has them all and more.

Monument Valley, Colorado

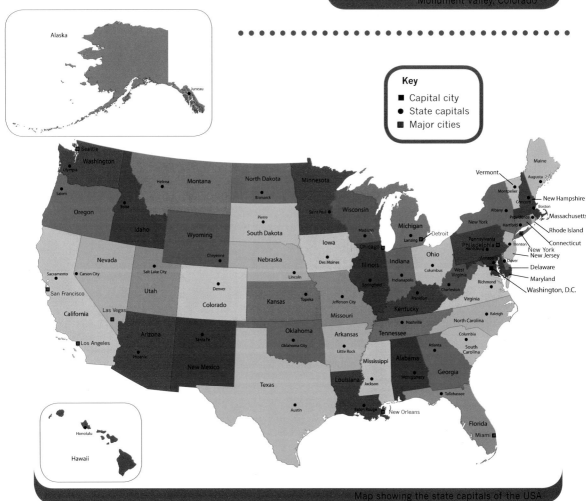

Key
■ Capital city
● State capitals
■ Major cities

Map showing the state capitals of the USA

CLIMATE

Most of the USA has summers warm enough for shorts, and winters cold enough for coats, hats and gloves. But to the south, parts of Florida are tropical all year, and there are baking-hot deserts in the southwest. Far to the north, Alaska has an Arctic climate.

LANDSCAPE

To the west, the Rocky Mountains are a magnet for thrill seekers, including snowboarders, skiers, climbers and mountain bikers. In the centre of the USA is a huge plain, and to the east are lower mountains and hills.

Landscape highlights to look out for:

- Geothermal geysers and hot springs in Yellowstone National Park
- The damp, dripping atmosphere of the Louisiana bayou wetlands
- Canyonlands National Park in Utah
- Towering cliffs in the Yosemite Valley, California

The Grand Prismatic Spring of Yellowstone National Park

WHAT IS THE USA?

USA is short for United States of America. It is made up of 50 states, 48 of them all together in a block. The other two are Alaska to the northwest, and Hawaii, a string of several islands in the middle of the Pacific Ocean.

FACT FILE ONE

CAPITAL CITY: Washington, D.C.

AREA: 9,161,966 km² of land area, plus 664,709 km² of sea area

HIGHEST MOUNTAIN: Mt McKinley (also called Denali) (6,194 m)

LOWEST POINT: Death Valley (-86 m)

LONGEST RIVER: Missouri (3,768 km)

BORDERS: Canada to the north, Mexico to the south

NATURAL HAZARDS: earthquakes, volcanoes, tsunamis, floods, hurricanes, tornadoes, wildfires

Chinese New Year celebrations in San Francisco

PEOPLE

Most Americans (almost four out of every five people) are descended from European immigrants. There are also large black and Hispanic communities, as well as many people from the Pacific and from Asia. Immigrants from all these places brought their music, festivals, cooking and more, giving the USA a rich cultural life.

URBAN LIFE

Already, four in every five Americans live in a town or city, and more are moving to urban areas each year. In the city centres, most people live in apartment buildings. Elsewhere, houses are more common. In the suburbs, people are used to living in large homes with gardens. Many cities – for example New York, San Francisco and Miami – are thriving with busy shops, cafés restaurants and music venues. A few, such as Detroit, are shrinking, as people are driven out by crime and lack of jobs.

Street café in Times Square, New York

RURAL LIFE

Agriculture is not a big employer in the USA: less than 1% of the workforce has a job in farming, fishing or forestry. Because work can be hard to find, some rural areas have become poor. Elsewhere, though, the tourist industry brings in millions of dollars each year. One example is New England, where the colourful displays of autumn leaves are a big attraction.

New England in the autumn

Chicago

FACT FILE TWO

POPULATION: 314 million

LARGEST CITIES/ CONURBATIONS: New York-Newark (19.3 million), Los Angeles-Long Beach-Santa Ana (12.7 million), Chicago (9.1 million), Miami (5.7 million), Washington, D.C. (4.4 million)

AGE STRUCTURE: 20% under 15 years old; 66.5% 15–64 years old; 13.5% over 64 years old

YOUTH UNEMPLOYMENT: (15–24 year-olds): 17.6%

OBESITY: 33.9%

LANGUAGES: There is no 'official' language for the USA, although some individual states list English as their official language. English is the first language of 82% of Americans; 11% of the population speak Spanish; 4% speak other European languages; and 3% speak Asian or Pacific languages

RELIGIONS: Christians make up 78.5% of the US population, Jews 1.7%; no other religion is followed by more than 1% of Americans

NEW YORK, N.Y.

In the 1800s, New York was the main place of arrival for **immigrants,** and today hundreds of different languages are still spoken here. New trends in fashion, art, music and culture spread from here around the USA (and around the world).

Breakdancing performance, New York City

THE FIVE BOROUGHS

New York City is actually made up of five boroughs, which combined in 1898 to make Greater New York.

The Bronx

The northernmost borough, where highlights include the Bronx Zoo and the nearby Botanical Gardens.

Insider tip: if you like Italian food, head for Arthur Avenue. Italian workers came here to build the zoo and the area is still jammed with Italian food sellers.

Brooklyn

Brooklyn is probably the hippest of the five boroughs, with amazing views from Brooklyn Heights to the skyscrapers of Manhattan.

Insider tip: head to Williamsburg, which is said to be the coolest part of Brooklyn, for people-watching and cutting-edge music venues.

Manhattan

Broadway's shops and the chance to rollerblade in Central Park (among other attractions) draw millions of visitors a year.

Insider tip: at the end of October, head for Washington Square's mind-boggling Village Halloween Parade.

Queens

Queens is very varied, with Greek, Mexican, Irish and Italian neighbourhoods.

Insider tip: head to Astoria for a screening at the Museum of the Moving Image, Greek food and vintage clothes shops.

Staten Island

Riding the free ferry from Manhattan to Staten Island, past the Statue of Liberty, is one of New York's great treats.

Insider tip: historic Richmond Town is a living museum of what life was like from the 1700s onward.

Crowds gather for Manhattan parade

"Once you have lived
in New York and it has
become your home,
no place else is good
enough."

— from *Second Helpings* by Megan
McCafferty

Overview of Manhattan and Brooklyn (on the far left)

SHOPPING –
THE INSIDE GUIDE

A great place to shop for leather goods

If you like to shop, there's nowhere like New York. Fifth Avenue, one of the city's most famous shopping streets, draws people from around the world. But there's a lot more to New York than this. Where should you head if you want something different to luxury boutiques and department stores?

SATURDAY SHOPPING TOUR

The best way to see New York City is on foot – but you won't want to walk around the whole five boroughs. Our tour is set in Manhattan, which is compact and easy to get around.

11:00 – Hester Street Fair
(April–October)
Start in the famous Lower East Side district. If you want quirky, whether it's clothing or food, from rare vintage outfits to ice-cream sandwiches, you'll probably find it here.

12:00 – The Market NYC
Next, head northwest to Bleecker Street, in Greenwich Village. The Market NYC is a treat for fashion followers: this is where New York's young designers come to sell their creations.

14:00 – Chelsea Market
If you're feeling hungry by now, head north – up Bleecker Street then 9th Avenue – to Chelsea Market. It's full of shops and stalls selling food from around the world.

15:30 – Malcolm Shabazz Harlem Market
Feeling refreshed? Still got energy for shopping? Catch the subway* north to 125th Street and head for the Harlem Market (above). Here you'll find a massive selection of African goods, including leather bags at distinctly non-designer prices.

*that's the local term for the underground train network.

FARMERS' MARKETS

Farmers' markets are a way for food growers to sell their products fresh, direct to the public. New York City has some great ones, including:

- **Union Square, Manhattan**
(Mon, Weds, Fri, Sat)
Started in 1976, this market has a great range of vegetables, meat, fish and bread.

- **Lincoln Center Greenmarket, Manhattan (right)**
(Thurs, Sat)
Check out the selection of organic food, vegetables, fruits and local specialities as well as crafts.

- **Borough Hall, Brooklyn**
(Tues, Thurs, Sat)
There's an Education Station that arranges educational tours and cooking demonstrations. The market is especially good for fresh vegetables, meat, fish and flowers.

Macy's, famous department store, at 34th Street and Broadway

APPLE CRAZY!

Wherever you go in the USA (in fact, wherever you go in the world), you see people using Apple computer products. Apple is a modern American success story – but it wasn't always like that. For most of the 1990s, Apple struggled to find people who wanted to buy its products.

APPLE TIMELINE

April Fool's Day, 1976: Apple is founded.

The company sold motherboards, which owners could build into a computer to their own design. At this time, computers didn't even have screens – let alone touchscreens.

1983: *Apple releases the first home computer with a screen*

A year later, in 1984, the first Apple Macintosh is released. It is announced using a now-famous advert directed by Ridley Scott (of *Alien*, *Blade Runner* and *Gladiator* fame).

1991: *The first PowerBook is released*

Despite the PowerBook's success, Apple begins to struggle. It develops products that don't sell well and loses customers.

1998: *The first iMac is introduced*

Designed by Jonathan Ive, who would later design the iPod and iPhone, the original iMac was a massive success.

2001: *the iPod*

The iPod digital music player was an even bigger success, and helped make Apple's fortune. Ten years later, Apple said it had sold 300 million iPods around the world.

2007: *the iPhone*

The iPhone has been leading the way ever since it was released, and grows increasingly popular. When the iPhone 5 was put on sale in 2012, over two million were sold within 24 hours.

2007: *the iPad*

Thousands of people around the world joined long queues, all hoping for the chance to be the first to own an iPad.

THE STORE THAT NEVER SLEEPS

If you're into Apple products, you'll want to visit the Apple Store on Fifth Avenue in Manhattan. And it doesn't matter what time of day or night you pick – it's open 24 hours a day, 365 days a year.

> **"A lot of times, people don't know what they want until you show it to them."**
>
> — Steve Jobs, one of the founders of Apple, describes the company's approach to developing new products

Early Apple Mac

The first Mac with a screen!

TECHNOLOGY AND TRANSPORT

FANTASTIC SUCCESS

By 2012, Apple was the world's second most valuable company. Its sales around the world came to $156 billion a year: that's greater than the entire economy of over half the countries in the world. Apple's profits were over $40 billion and 53% of its revenue that year came from the sale of 37 million iPhones (right).

CAR CRAZY!

Most journeys in the USA are made by car. Whether going shopping, visiting a beauty spot or heading out for a meal, you usually drive. Outside the cities, many people live a long way from shops, schools and work, so their cars are important to them.

Rally for custom and vintage cars

"For the most part, Americans without cars are very young, very old, disabled or live in Manhattan."

— Daniel Sperling and Deborah Gordon, *Two Billion Cars*

DRIVING REGULATIONS

In most states, you can get a driving licence at 16 years of age. In some states you have to be 18 or 21.

A classic 'Chevy' (Chevrolet) convertible

TRAFFIC

Today, there are about 150 million cars in the USA: one for every two Americans (including children and other people who don't drive). As a result, many roads in and around cities are extremely busy. City centres regularly suffer from 'gridlock', which is when there's so much traffic that none of it moves. When you DO get to where you're going, finding somewhere to park is often tricky.

YOUNG PEOPLE AND CARS

These days, young Americans are using cars less than they did in the past. Cost, traffic and parking problems, and concern for the environment have all made driving less attractive. Instead, young people use a combination of walking, bicycles and public transport. Doing this has become easier in some US states. In California, for example, you can load your bike on to the front of a bus.

Many cities suffer from traffic trouble

BIKE CULTURE, PORTLAND STYLE

If you like to bike, take a visit to Portland, Oregon. It has the highest percentage of cyclists anywhere in the USA. Bike highlights include:

The Naked Bike Ride in June:
thousands of naked people cycle through the city

Worst Day of the Year Ride:
one weekend in February, 4,000 riders pedal through the winter gloom, dreaming of summer

AMERICA'S FAVOURITE FOODS

There's nowhere quite like the USA for foodies.
Whatever kind of cooking you want, you'll be able to find it in most cities and towns. If you fancy a Jewish breakfast, a lobster roll, enchiladas, posh French-style cooking or something – anything – else, you'll probably be able to find it.

Corn dogs are hot dogs fried in corn batter

TOP 10 FOODS

A not-100%-scientific survey came up with this list of the USA's favourite foods:

1. Thanksgiving Dinner (see page 22)
2. Cheeseburger
3. Reuben sandwich (see page 21)
4. Hot dogs
5. Philly cheese steak (a sandwich made from thinly sliced pieces of steak and melted cheese in a long roll)
6. Nachos (see page 21)
7. Chicago-style pizza (see page 21)
8. Delmonico's steak (a specially prepared beef steak)
9. Blueberry cobbler (cooked fruit with a sort of crumbled pie topping)
10. Chocolate-chip cookies

TOP DISHES, AND A BIT OF HISTORY

These favourite dishes are also a guide to the immigrants who built the USA:

The northeast:
Reuben sandwich

A hot sandwich with corned beef, sauerkraut, Swiss cheese and a dressing. Invented by either a Lithuanian grocer or a German deli owner (depending on who you believe) in the early 1900s.

> **"Reuben, make me a sandwich... I'm so hungry I could eat a brick."**
>
> — famished actress Anna Selos, whose order apparently led to the invention of the Reuben sandwich

The Midwest:
Chicago-style pizza

This is a deep-dish pizza with a thick crust. It's an American version of the thinner pizzas first brought to the USA by Italian immigrants. They arrived in the late 1800s and early 1900s, and Italian restaurants soon became popular in many US cities.

The southeast:
Jambalaya

Jambalaya is a stew of meat, vegetables and rice. It was brought to the USA from the Caribbean. Jambalaya was originally developed as a combination of French, Spanish and Caribbean cooking in the early 1800s.

The southwest:
Nachos

Nachos originally developed in Mexico – which between 1769 and 1848 owned a big chunk of the western USA. Today they are popular with almost everyone, not only Mexican-Americans. Nachos are usually served with cheese and hot chilli peppers. They also often come with guacamole or salsa.

FOOD

Reuben sandwich

Cajun jambalaya

THANKSGIVING: THE USA'S NO.1 HOLIDAY

Thanksgiving Dinner

Most Americans work long hours. They also get less holiday time than people in Europe, with few people able to take more than two weeks off each year. As a result, Americans make the most of public holidays and long weekends.

THANKSGIVING

Thanksgiving is the No.1 holiday weekend in the USA. It's a celebration of family and friends. Mums, dads, brothers, sisters, grandparents and other family make a special effort to get together for one of the highlights of the year – Thanksgiving Day Dinner. As a result, in the days leading up to Thanksgiving, the roads, railways and airports are always jammed with people.

THANKSGIVING DINNER

If you're lucky enough to be invited to an American family's Thanksgiving Dinner, it might be best if you don't eat breakfast that day. This is a giant meal! You can expect to be fed most of the following:

Turkey

Turkey has been part of Thanksgiving since the very beginning, when early settlers found wild turkeys everywhere. The turkey is usually filled with stuffing (a mixture of bread and herbs is traditional) and served with gravy.

Side dishes

Mashed potato, winter squash, sweet potatoes/yams, corn-on-the-cob, cranberry sauce, green beans, peas and carrots.

Pudding

Some sort of pie is traditional: fillings include pumpkin, sweet potato, apple and pecan. The pie is usually served with cream, ice cream – or both.

> **"You can tell you ate too much for Thanksgiving when you have to let your bathrobe out."**
>
> — US talk show host Jay Leno

PUBLIC HOLIDAYS

HOLIDAY:	
New Year's Day: *1 January*	
Martin Luther King Jr Day: *3rd Monday of January*	Celebrates the famous civil rights leader
Presidents' Day/Washington's Birthday: *3rd Monday of February*	People remember past presidents
Memorial Day: *Last Monday in May*	People remember those who have died in the US armed forces
Independence Day: *4 July*	Celebration of the USA's independence from Great Britain
Labor Day: *1st Monday in September*	In honour of ordinary American working people
Columbus Day: *2nd Monday in October*	Celebrates the arrival of Christopher Columbus on the shores of North America
Veterans' Day: *11 November*	Honours those who have fought for the USA in wars
Thanksgiving: *4th Thursday in November*	
Christmas Day: *25th December*	

FOOD

Typical Thanksgiving ingredients

NEW-WORLD DINNER

The 'First Thanksgiving' was a meal between settlers and American Indians in 1621. Ever since, traditional Thanksgiving dinners have included lots of foods that are native to North America.

MUSIC MAP OF **AMERICA**

US rock band Phish at the Bonnaroo Festival (p. 27)

T he USA is a joy for music lovers. True, the radio plays lots of predictable, middle-of-the-road sounds. But if you dig a little deeper, there are all kinds of musical treasures. Many kinds of music are associated with particular areas.

AMERICAN MUSICAL MOVIES

Enchanted (2007)
Features Giselle, a typical Disney Princess, who is forced from her traditional animated world into the live-action world of New York City.

Boyz N The Hood (1991)
The soundtrack for this Los Angeles-set movie features some of the big stars of the 90s rap scene: Ice Cube, 2 Live Crew and more.

This Is Spinal Tap (1984)
Several real-life rock bands have said how this spoof movie about a (made-up) rock band's tour of the USA is realistic.

The Blues Brothers (1980)
Even if you don't like blues music, the famous car chase through Chicago is a good reason to watch this.

MUSIC HOTSPOTS IN THE USA

DETROIT – MOTOWN, THEN INDIE

Back in the 1960s, the Motown record label sprang up and took the world by storm with its poppy soul music. Later, in the 2000s, the distorted rock pioneered by The White Stripes grew up in Detroit.

SEATTLE – GRUNGE

Grunge was made famous in the 1990s by bands such as Nirvana and Pearl Jam. Today, bands like the Smashing Pumpkins and Soundgarden keep the sound alive.

Seattle
Olympia
Washington
Salem
Oregon
Hele
Idaho
Boise
.Paul
Wisconsin
Madison
Michigan
Lansing
Detroit
Iowa
Chicago
Carson City
Salt Lake City
Cheyenne
Nebraska
Des Moines
Ohio
Nevada
Lincoln
Illinois
Indiana
Columbus
Denver
Springfield
Indianapolis
California
Las Vegas
Colorado
Topeka
St. Louis
Frankfort
Los Angeles
Arizona
Santa Fe
Jefferson City
Kentucky
Phoenix
New Mexico
Kansas
Missouri
Nashville
Oklahoma
Tenessee
Oklahoma City
Arkansas
Memphis
Little Rock
Atlanta
Dallas
Mississippi
Montgome
Georgia
Jackson
Texas
Louisiana
Alabam
Austin
Baton Rouge
Tallahass
Houston
New Orlea
Fl

CULTURE

LOS ANGELES – ROCK AND RAP

Rock bands Guns N' Roses (whose *Appetite for Destruction* is the best-selling debut album ever), Red Hot Chilli Peppers and Linkin Park all developed here. From across town came rappers such as Dr Dre, Ice Cube and Snoop Dogg.

ATLANTA – HIP-HOP AND R&B

Home to many big stars, including Cee Lo Green, B.o.B., and Outkast, this is a great place to see live acts.

MUSIC FESTIVALS

Wherever you go in the USA, you probably won't be far from a music festival, especially in the summertime. Small ones, where you can get close to the performers, are advertised in local papers, coffee shops and diners. Bigger festivals are advertised nationwide, and it can be tricky to get tickets. If there's a particular festival you want to see, book ahead.

Live rap at South by Southwest

SOUTH BY SOUTHWEST

South by Southwest is held in and around Austin, Texas in March. This is a great time to visit Austin as it's when the area's famous spring wildflowers begin to appear.

The music is part of a bigger festival, which also has comedy, interactive and film events, so there's plenty to see. There are over 100 music venues spread around the city: you could listen to 50 Cent rapping in a church at lunchtime, then head to a city park to listen to Mumford & Sons.

OTHER THINGS TO DO IN TEXAS IN MARCH

Houston Livestock Show and Rodeo:
Over two million people can't be wrong! This is said to be the world's biggest rodeo.

Sweetwater Rattlesnake Roundup:
Because how many times will you get the chance to have fried rattlesnake for lunch?

North Texas Irish Festival:
Texas won't seem such a strange place for an Irish festival once the pipe and drum bands get going.

OTHER MUSIC FESTIVALS

Here are just a few insider tips for some of the USA's top festivals:

APRIL:

Coachella
(Indio, California)
Known for its combination of new, established and re-formed groups. Take a hat and sunscreen, though: the temperature regularly breaks 40°C.

JUNE:

Bonnaroo
(Manchester, Tennessee)
You name it, you can probably hear it at Bonnaroo, from indie to hip hop, gospel, Americana and rock.

JUNE–JULY:

Summerfest
(Milwaukee, Wisconsin)
Also known as The Big Gig, because it's officially the biggest music festival in the world, with every kind of music you can think of.

AUGUST:

Lollapalooza
(Chicago, Illinois)
Lollapalooza always has a great mix of acts. There's a bicycle park, farmers' market, shopping area and food stalls too.

Welcome to the world's biggest music festival

L.A. AND HOLLYWOOD

The famous Hollywood sign – 14 metres high

Los Angeles beach-house party

The West Coast, as the Pacific edge of America is known, is famous for its sunshine and high-energy, fun lifestyle. For a taste of everything the West Coast has to offer, take a trip to Los Angeles – also known as the City of Angels.

L.A. MOVIES

The Muppets (2010)

The story of how two brothers help Kermit the Frog reunite the Muppets and save the Muppet Theater in Los Angeles from being knocked down.

Dogtown and Z-Boys (2001)

The story of the 1970s Zephyr skateboard team has great L.A. atmosphere.

Rebel Without a Cause (1955)

A rebellious kid moves to L.A. – a great story, with amazing shots of the city in the 1950s.

Speed (1994)

A bus zooms around L.A. trying to keep above 50 mph: otherwise, a bomb on board will go off.

TAKE THE L.A. HAUNTED TOUR

Lots of companies offer tours of L.A. You can take tours to famous people's homes, tourist sites, even places where famous crimes have happened. This tour, though, is a tour with a difference...

Stop 1: Hollywood Roosevelt Hotel

Phantom calls from empty rooms, lights and taps that mysteriously turn on – and celebrity ghosts! They say Marilyn Monroe (1926–62) used to appear in a mirror in the lobby, and guests still hear Montgomery Clift (1920–1966) playing his trumpet – even though he died in 1966.

Stop 2: Griffith Park

When a young woman was cheated out of this land in the late 1800s, she cursed all future owners. The girl is still reported to ride the trails at night, wearing a white dress and astride a ghost horse.

Stop 3: Pantages Theater

Haunted by the ghost of movie mogul Howard Hughes, an oddball who liked to sort his peas by size and insisted his employees shouldn't look at him. Hughes is apparently STILL looking over workers' shoulders to check they're doing things properly, which must make it hard to concentrate.

The Hollywood walk of fame

> " Hollywood is a cross between a health farm, a recreation centre and an insane asylum."
>
> — Michael Caine

CULTURE

HOLLYWOOD

There can't be many people in the world who haven't heard of Hollywood. It's an area in Los Angeles where the US film industry was traditionally based. Many of the world's biggest film studios are still based here.

Filming in Hollywood

NATIONAL SPORTS

The USA has three big national sports: American football, baseball and basketball. Ice hockey is also very popular. Once in a while, each of these sports captures the attention of even non-sports fans, in the same way as the FA Cup final does in England.

A college American football game in New York

LIVE AND ON TV

Heading to a stadium to watch a contest is great fun. Aside from the sports action there are cheerleaders, half-time shows and food sellers. Watching a big game on TV with a group of Americans is almost as much fun, with a rowdy party atmosphere, food and drink.

Here's our guide to the big games in each of the three sports:

American football

In February, Super Bowl Sunday decides the year's champion team. So many people sit down to watch that, in effect, it's a national holiday for most Americans.

Baseball

In October, the top two Major League baseball teams fight out the World Series. They play up to seven games, with the first to notch up four wins taking the title.

Basketball

In June, the NBA (National Basketball Association) Finals see the top two teams play a best-of-seven series to decide the champions. Almost as popular as the NBA championship matches is the 'March Madness' college basketball tournament. Played mostly in March, this is one of the most popular TV sports events in the USA.

THE TAILGATE PARTY

The tailgate party (below) is a big favourite with US sports fans. They arrive hours early at the stadium and turn the car park into a massive picnic and barbecue area.

CELEBRITY BASKETBALL FANS

Basketball is popular with celebrities. Many NBA teams have one or two actors, musicians or celebrities in the front row, including:

LA Lakers: David Beckham, Jack Nicholson, Leonardo di Caprio, Chris Rock

New York Knicks: Spike Lee

New Jersey Nets: Jay-Z

Boston Celtics: Matt Damon

Tailgate party in the sunshine, Pittsburgh

SPORT

A DAY AT THE RODEO

Rodeo stunt riding

What could be more American than a rodeo? The events in a rodeo are based on the old-time skills of cowboys, and you'll see plenty of cowboy boots and Stetson hats in the audience! These days, rodeo is not only entertainment, but also a competitive sport.

CHEYENNE FRONTIER DAYS

Cheyenne Frontier Days in Cheyenne, Wyoming is known to rodeo fans as 'The Daddy Of 'Em All'. First held in 1896, Frontier Days is now more than simply a rodeo – it's a week-long festival of everything Western, including music, art, a Wild West show and a Native American village.

So, what are the events particularly worth watching out for?

Tie-down roping

Riders have to lasso a calf, dismount, pull the calf over and tie it up so that it can't move.

Saddle and bareback bronco riding

Riders try to stay on an untrained, bucking horse for as long as possible. As if that's not hard enough, these days the horses are specially bred for their bucking ability.

Bull riding

Bulls don't like being ridden, and it's not easy to stay on one for eight seconds. If you manage that, you still have to get off and escape from the rodeo ring.

Barrel racing

Fast, amazingly agile horses are ridden round a twisting course at high speed.

> **"It's all or nothing, and the number one thing is – you cannot ride timid."**
>
> — multiple world champion barrel racer, Charmayne James

In hot pursuit of an escaping calf

OTHER TOP RODEOS

Lauglin River Stampede, Nevada

A rodeo with more of a small-town feel, but still great quality riders.

La Fiesta de los Vaqueros, Arizona

This rodeo is named for the vaqueros, old-time Mexican cowboys. Many vaqueros worked in the American South West.

National Finals Rodeo, Nevada

The 15 best male and female rodeo riders in the USA compete to see who will come out on top.

Rocky Mountain Stampede, Colorado

The Rocky Mountain town of Greeley hosts a rodeo, music concerts, art shows, barbecues and a parade.

A VISIT TO THE SUPER-VOLCANO

Lying underneath part of the USA is a ticking volcanic bomb, which some scientists think will one day destroy all life on Earth. It's a super-volcano, and it's underneath the Yellowstone National Park. Fortunately there's no sign of a super-eruption any time soon* – so for now, the park is safe to visit.

*Although an eruption is several thousand years overdue.

National park wilderness

A Yellowstone geyser

GEYSER CENTRAL

One of the biggest highlights of a trip to Yellowstone is the park's geysers. These holes in the ground regularly squirt massive jets of hot water up into the air. There are more geysers in Yellowstone than anywhere else in the world.

HOT SPRINGS

There are hot springs dotted around Yellowstone, but some of the most amazing are at Mammoth. Here, the water has left behind a chalky-white mineral that looks like milk boiling over from a pan. It might look like a nice place for a warm bath, but DO NOT go in! People and animals have died after entering Yellowstone's hot springs, burned by the extreme temperatures.

ANIMAL SPOTTING IN YELLOWSTONE

Yellowstone is a haven for animals. Here are just a few you might be lucky enough to spot:

- Black bears and grizzly bears
- Bison (right); Watch out! Bison are said to kill more visitors each year than bears
- Bobcats and lynx (though both are extremely rare)
- Mountain lions
- Wolves

"Break away, once in awhile, and climb a mountain or spend a week in the woods."
— John Muir, one of the key campaigners who helped to establish America's national parks

INSIDER TIP: THREE NATIONAL PARKS

Many parks are less well known than famous ones such as Yellowstone. Here are three insider tips:

Acadia (Maine)
Far up the Atlantic coast of the USA, this quiet park is a good place for imagining what life must have been like for the settlers in the 1600s.

Bryce Canyon (Utah)
The red rock formations include amazing spires called 'hoodoos', twisting canyons and other amazing shapes.

Grand Teton (Wyoming)
Brilliant for keen naturalists: bison, black bears, golden eagles and moose can all be spotted.

ON AN ADVENTURE

RAFTING THE GRAND CANYON

Twists and turns of the Grand Canyon in Arizona

The Grand Canyon is one of the great wonders of the natural world. It consistently appears on lists of the best places to visit in the USA. Standing on the edge looking down is amazing enough – but to get a real feel for the canyon, what could be better than rafting down it? The trip down the 84 km of the Lower Gorge is one of the most popular, and takes between two and five days.

RAFTING THE GRAND CANYON: A GUIDE

You can't just turn up and catch a raft down the Grand Canyon. The easiest way to make the trip is to book it with an official guiding company.

1: Putting your raft in the water

Access the river at Diamond Creek. To get there, you cross land belonging to the Hualapai tribe of American Indians.

2: Paddle!

From Diamond Creek the next 84 km of river, all the way to the finish at Lake Mead, is free-flowing white water.

3: Camp!

The trip down this stretch of river, which is called the Lower Gorge, takes up to five days. Setting up camp and going to sleep with the river roaring nearby, and the sides of the canyon towering above you, is an amazing experience.

GRAND CANYON SURVIVAL CHECKLIST

✓ Tie up your raft securely. If it floats away, you're in big trouble!

✓ Bring sun cream and enough food and water, plus a little extra in case you are delayed.

✓ Always camp above the high-water mark (shown by the line of twigs and leaves the river has left behind).

Mountain bike action in Durango, Colorado

EXTREME FUN IN THE USA

If the Grand Canyon makes you want to see more extreme action, here are some other places to visit:

Yosemite National Park, California

The best place to see people rock climbing up giant cliffs that take days to scale

North Shore, Hawaii

Surfers from all over the world arrive here in winter to take on the huge, powerful waves

Thompson Pass, Alaska

The place to catch some of the most extreme, steepest snowboarding anywhere in the world

Durango, Colorado

One of the best mountain-biking venues anywhere on Planet Earth (above)

ON AN ADVENTURE

ALASKA

Alaska is the largest state in the USA, but has fewer people per square kilometre than any other. Under a million people live in Alaska permanently.* If you want wilderness, this is the place to come!

*There are greater numbers of native peoples here than in most other parts of the USA: roughly 15% of the population are American Indians or Alaskan Natives.

In the far north, it pays to dress for the cold, as the Alaskan natives do

ALASKA HIGHLIGHTS

In Alaska, there are hundreds of ways to enjoy the stunning natural environment. Here are a few tips for things to do:

Visit Kodiak Island

Take a bear-spotting flight (the island is famous for its bears), hike on the local trails, or visit the Alutiiq Museum to find out about the native people of the area.

Watch the Kuskokwim 300 dog-sled race

Each January, some of the world's top 'mushers' race their dog-sleds along the old mail route on the Kuskokwim River (right). The race is over 300 miles (480 km) and has prize money of $100,000.

Head for the Kenai Peninsula

You can visit Russian Orthodox church buildings, which were built from the 1840s – when Russia, not the USA, owned Alaska. (The state was bought from the Russians in 1867.) You can sometimes spot whales off the coast. You may also see the biggest salmon on the planet, which migrate each summer into the Kenai and Russian Rivers.

Check out the totem poles in Ketchican

Alaska is famous for the carved totem poles its native people make, and Ketchican has lots to see. In summer the town also holds a logging show, with log rolling on the water, axe-throwing, chopping and tree-climbing contests.

THE ENVIRONMENT

Alaska is rich in natural resources: oil and gas exploration and logging have brought money to the state. They have also brought deforestation, oil spills and other environmental problems. Many groups now campaign to limit damage to the environment.

FISHING – FOR GOLD

The town of Nome, Alaska is so remote that there is no road to it. Even so, people come here every summer to dredge gold from the sand off its beaches. Some estimates say that there are millions of dollars in gold still in the sands.

ON AN ADVENTURE

Dog-sled racing

THE HAWAIIAN ISLANDS

When you think of the USA, you probably don't imagine Pacific islands, palm trees and sandy beaches – but there is a part of the USA you can visit to experience these. It's the state of Hawaii, far out in the Pacific Ocean.

Surfboards for rent, Waikiki Beach

ISLANDS BUILT BY VOLCANO

The Hawaiian Islands were formed by a volcanic 'hot spot' on the floor of the Pacific Ocean. The hot spot is still active and causes new eruptions every day. Hawaii is one of the few places anywhere that people can get close to an active volcano. The big three are:

Mauna Loa – which hasn't erupted since 1984. Mauna Loa is one of the 16 Decade Volcanos, which are watched especially closely by scientists. This is because if it erupted, the lives of thousands of people would be at risk.

Kilauea – which has been erupting continually since 1983 (but which is still great fun to mountain-bike down!).

Loihi – an underwater volcano that has been erupting since 1996, and is forecast to break the surface in about 250,000 years.

Kilauea erupts

THE BIRTHPLACE OF SURFING

Hawaii is famous around the world as the place where surfing was invented. A Hawaiian lifeguard called George Freeth took surfing to California in 1907. Hawaii's champion swimmer and surfer Duke Kahanamoku first demonstrated it in Australia in 1915.

SURF ETIQUETTE

A few things to know if you want to give surfing a try:

1. Any surfer riding in must steer around surfers paddling out.

2. The surfer closest to the whitewater has the right to ride the wave alone.

3. Don't paddle in front of someone trying to catch a wave.

HAWAII'S PEOPLE

The first settlers in Hawaii were the Native Hawaiians. They were Polynesian voyagers, who journeyed vast distances in sea-going canoes, across open ocean far from the sight of land, to reach Hawaii. Over a thousand years later, in the late 1700s, Europeans began to arrive. They were followed by Americans, Japanese, Filipinos, Chinese and finally more Pacific Islanders, following hundreds of years later in the footsteps of their ancestors. The food, music and culture of the islands show all these influences. You can eat fantastic sushi, listen to ukulele music and play a game of baseball all on the same day!

ON AN ADVENTURE

Ukulele lesson on a black-sand Haiwaiian beach

KEY INFORMATION
FOR TRAVELLERS

LANGUAGE

English is spoken everywhere, though the USA has no official national language. Spanish is widely spoken, especially in southern states such as California, New Mexico, Texas and Florida.

ENTERING THE USA

US immigration officials are very strict. Almost all visitors to the USA must have a visa: without one, you will not be allowed into the country. People from some countries, for example the United Kingdom, can apply for an Electronic Travel Authority online before they travel.

Other visitors may have to contact their local US Embassy. Your government will have information on requirements for travel to the USA.

GETTING AROUND

The USA has a railway system connecting cities and towns, but away from the East Coast, train journeys can be long because of the distances involved. Many people prefer to fly. Buses run in large cities and towns. Cycling is encouraged in some cities and areas: Oregon and California have made special efforts to encourage cycling.

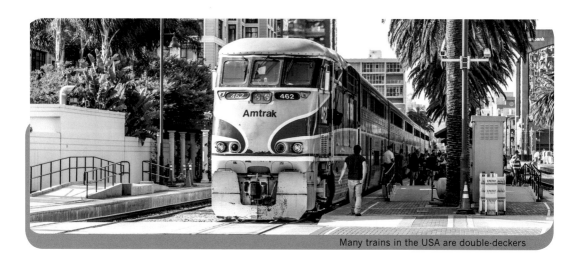

Many trains in the USA are double-deckers

HEALTH

If you have a minor health problem such as a sore throat, a pharmacy could be a good source of help.

Visitors who need to be treated by a doctor will almost certainly have to pay, as public healthcare is only really available to the very poor. Medical treatment is very expensive, so it's important to have good travel insurance.

POSTAL SERVICES

The main postal service is the United States Postal Service. You can buy stamps at post offices and at stamp machines in hotels and other locations.

Letters can be posted at a post office, or in the postboxes that are a common sight on street corners. Usually they are dark blue, and they have 'United States Postal Service' on a white panel on the sides.

MOBILE NETWORKS

Foreign mobile phones do not usually work in the USA. If you need a mobile during your visit, it is possible to hire one, or pre-paid phones can be bought from many stores. Smartphones will work on WiFi, but will not work using the US mobile network.

INTERNET PROVISION

The USA generally has good Internet provision. Free WiFi zones are available in many public spaces, hotels and cafés. Internet cafés offer paid Internet access and computer use.

NATURAL HAZARDS

From June to November, hurricanes can affect the southern and western coasts of the USA: there is usually plenty of warning if a hurricane is coming.

From March to November, dryer areas are at risk from forest fires, particularly on the West Coast.

A hurricane in Miami, Florida, during hurricane season

THE ESSENTIALS

CURRENCY:

Dollar ($) ($1 = roughly £0.66, or €0.76). You can change money at larger banks, and at currency exchange counters on city streets. You can also use a foreign bankcard in many American cash machines.

TIME ZONE:

Standard Time is GMT -5 or 6 hours, but the 50 states cover six different time zones. On the second Sunday in March, Daylight Saving Time begins, and clocks are put forward one hour. On the first Sunday in November clocks go back to Standard Time.

TELEPHONE DIALLING CODES:

To call the USA from outside the country, add 00 1 to the beginning of the number, and drop the zero.

To call another country from the USA, add 00 and the country code of the place you are dialling to the beginning of the number, and drop the zero.

OPENING HOURS:

In cities and towns, most shops are open by 10:00 and closed by 21:00 from Monday to Saturday. On Sundays, they are usually open between 11:00 and 17:00. Supermarkets are open for much longer, for example from 07:00 to 23:00; a few stay open 24 hours a day, 7 days a week.

In rural areas, shops are generally open 09:00–18:00, but may be closed all day on Sunday.

AMERICAN ENGLISH:

There are quite a few words that are different in the USA. It's worth knowing them – or you may be disappointed when you order 'chips' and a bag of crisps arrives.

UK	USA	UK	USA	UK	USA
biscuit	cookie	chips	french fries	queue	line
sweets	candy	bill	check	pavement	sidewalk
courgette	zucchini	underground	subway	pants	underwear
ice lolly	popsicle	petrol	gas	trousers	pants
crisps	chips	zebra crossing/ pedestrian crossing	crosswalk		

FINDING OUT MORE

BOOKS TO READ: NON-FICTION

Countries in Our World: USA Lisa Klobuchar (Franklin Watts, 2012)
This book examines the USA's physical features, daily life, industry, media, leisure and much more.

The United States of America: a State-by-State Guide Millie Miller and Cyndi Nelson (Scholastic, 2006)

Contains basic information about every one of the 50 states. If you want to know the state flower of Minnesota, the main crops grown in Iowa, which species are endangered in Florida, or a thousand other facts, this is the place to look.

Field Guide to North American Mammals Audubon Society (Random House, first edition 1998)
Hundreds of colour photographs, plus information on the habitat, behaviour, and tracks of each animal, make this an excellent book for nature lovers. It is part of a series covering everything from insects to seashells.

BOOKS TO READ: FICTION

The Absolutely True Diary of a Part-Time Indian Sherman Alexie
The story of Junior, and what happens when he leaves the Spokane Indian Reservation to go to an off-reservation, all-white high school.

The Call of the Wild Jack London
A classic book for young people, *Call of the Wild* is about a crossbreed dog called Buck, who is kidnapped and taken to work as a sled dog in the Yukon. After many adventures, Buck eventually goes back to the wild, and becomes the leader of a wolf pack.

The Adventures of Huckleberry Finn Mark Twain
Huck decides it's time to run away in the company of escaped slave Jim. They float off together down the Mississippi River on a raft, and have many adventures – some comic, some scary.

WEBSITES

www.discoveramerica.com
Packed with information, this is a great site for starting to plan a trip to the USA. Clicking on the 'States and Cities' tab takes you to a list of all 50 states. Click on a state name and you'll see ideas for places to visit, surprising facts, top sights and much more.

https://www.cia.gov/library/publications/the-world-factbook/geos/uk.html
This link will take you to the CIA (Central Intelligence Agency) web page about the United Kingdom. It's quite dry, but crammed full of useful information and statistics.

Note to parents and teachers:
Every effort has been made by the Publishers to ensure that these websites are suitable for children, that they are of the highest educational value, and that they contain no inappropriate or offensive material. However, because of the nature of the Internet, it is impossible to guarantee that the contents of these sites will not be altered. We strongly advise that Internet access is supervised by a responsible adult.

THE ESSENTIALS

INDEX

Alaska 9, 37, 38–39
American English 44
American football 30
American Indians 23, 32, 36, 38
Apple (computers etc) 16–17
Atlanta 25

baseball 30, 41
basketball 30, 31
beaches 7, 8, 39, 40, 41
Bonnaroo 24, 27
borders 9
Boyz N The Hood 24

cars 7, 18–19
Chicago 7, 11, 21, 24
climate 9
Coachella 27
Colorado 8, 33, 37
countryside
cowboys 6, 32, 33
currency 44
cycling 7, 19, 27, 37, 42

Detroit 10, 25
Dogtown and Z-Boys 28

Enchanted 24

film industry 6, 28–29
food 6, 7, 12, 14, 15, 20–23, 27

geysers 9, 34
Grand Canyon 7, 36–37

Halloween 6, 12, 13
Hawaiian Islands 7, 9, 37, 40–41
healthcare 43
holidays 22, 23
Hollywood 6, 7, 28–29
Honolulu 7
housing 10
hurricanes 9, 43

immigration/immigrants 10, 12, 21, 41, 42

Jobs, Steve 17

landscape 6, 8–9
languages 11, 12, 42
Lolapalooza 27
Los Angeles 6, 7, 11, 24, 25, 28–29

Manhattan 6, 12, 13, 14, 15, 17, 18
markets 14, 15, 27
Miami 10, 11, 43
mountains 9, 35
movies 6, 24, 28, 29
music 6, 10, 12, 24–27, 32, 33
    festivals 6, 26–27

Naked Bike Ride 7, 19
national parks 9, 34, 35, 37
New England 11
New Orleans 7
New York/New York City 7, 10, 11, 12–15, 24, 30, 31

Oregon 7, 19, 42

population 11
post (postal service) 43

rafting 7, 36, 37
Rebel Without a Cause 28
religion 11
Rocky Mountains 9, 33
rodeo 6, 26, 32–33
rural life 11

San Francisco 7, 10
Seattle 25
shopping (New York) 14–15
South by Southwest 6, 26

Speed 28
sport 6, 30–33
Summerfest 27
surfing 7, 37, 40, 41

telephones 43, 44
Texas 6, 26
Thanksgiving 20, 22–23
The Blues Brothers 24
The Muppets 28
This is Spinal Tap 24
transport 18–19, 42

US States 8, 9

visas 42
volcanoes 9, 34, 40

Washington D.C. 9, 11
work 10, 11, 18, 22

Yellowstone National Park 9, 34–35
Yosemite National Park 9, 37